# DRUGS AND DRUG ABUSE

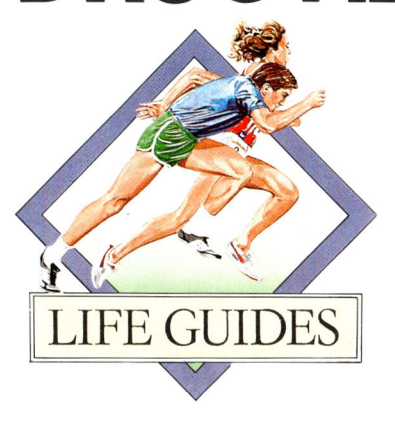

**LIFE GUIDES**

# DRUGS AND DRUG ABUSE

### Brian R. Ward

Series consultant:
**Dr Alan Maryon-Davis**
MB, BChir, MSc, MRCP, FFCM

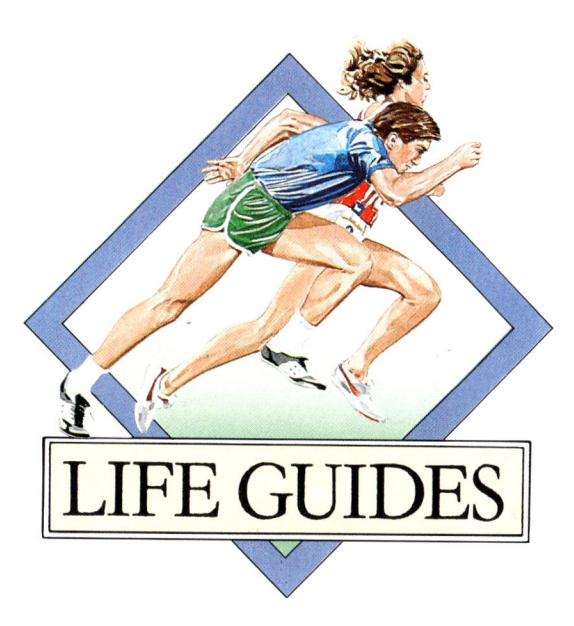

**LIFE GUIDES**

**Franklin Watts**
London · New York · Toronto · Sydney

© 1987 Franklin Watts

First published in Great Britain in 1987 by
Franklin Watts
12a Golden Square, London W1

First published in the USA by
Franklin Watts Inc.
387 Park Avenue South
New York, N.Y. 10016

First published in Australia by
Franklin Watts Australia
14 Mars Road, Lane Cove
New South Wales 2066

UK ISBN: 086313 502 1
US ISBN: 0-531-10358-7
Library of Congress Catalog Card No: 86-51412

Design: Howard Dyke

Picture research: Anne-Marie Ehrlich

Illustrations: Dick Bonson, Howard Dyke, Sally Launder, David Mallott.

Photographs:
Department of Health and Social Security 7*b*
Mark Edwards 13
Hutchison Library 21*t*, 23, 27, 30
Impact Photos 15, 29; National Lifeline 37
Mike Newton 8–9, 10–11, 21*b*, 35
Rex Features 17, 25, 31, 36, 44, 45
Science Photo Library 28
Scottish Health Education Group 7*t*
John Watney 43; Dr Joyce Watson 18
ZEFA 33, 39

Printed in Belgium

# Contents

| | |
|---|---|
| Introduction | 6 |
| Medical drugs | 8 |
| Everyday drugs | 10 |
| Addiction | 12 |
| The drug habit | 14 |
| The social effects of drug taking | 16 |
| Glues and solvents | 18 |
| Cannabis | 20 |
| Cocaine | 22 |
| Crack: a new threat | 24 |
| Heroin | 26 |
| The effects of heroin | 28 |
| Drugs and organized crime | 30 |
| Tranquillizers | 32 |
| Uppers and downers | 34 |
| LSD | 36 |
| Drugs outside the law | 38 |
| Recognizing a drug problem | 40 |
| What to do if a friend is taking drugs | 42 |
| Getting off drugs | 44 |
| Glossary | 46 |
| Where to go for help | 47 |
| Index | 48 |

# Introduction

Drug use is recognized as a growing threat to young people in many countries. Every day more and more people try drugs. Many will continue to use them until their physical and mental health are affected.

Drugs are substances which affect the body or the mind in some way. At first they can produce a pleasant effect, but very quickly, they may cause lasting damage to the mind and body. This is why experimenting with drugs is so dangerous.

Most regular drug users risk some type of mental or physical damage from the drugs, or from the methods they use to take them. Many people become dependent on or addicted to their drugs and are unable to cope with life without them. Illegal drugs offered for sale are very often contaminated, so the effects of taking a drug are unpredictable. And because use and possession of most drugs is illegal, drug usage leads people into trouble with the law.

In this book we shall look at many different types of drugs, their effects and health risks, and try to find out why people start to take them.

Young people who are offered drugs can always choose to say no. This is the message of many of the anti-drug campaigns and information published by governments and health authorities.

Posters such as this aim to shock by showing the serious physical effects of drug taking. Drug abuse causes general ill health as well as more serious physical and emotional problems.

# Medical drugs

The drugs used in medicine today have been produced to solve particular medical problems. Some treat diseases of the body, while others affect the mind.

Such drugs are useful when given for the purpose for which they were developed, under the supervision of a doctor. They can only be supplied with a doctor's prescription, so that their use can be properly controlled.

But even medical drugs can be dangerous when misused. Some can

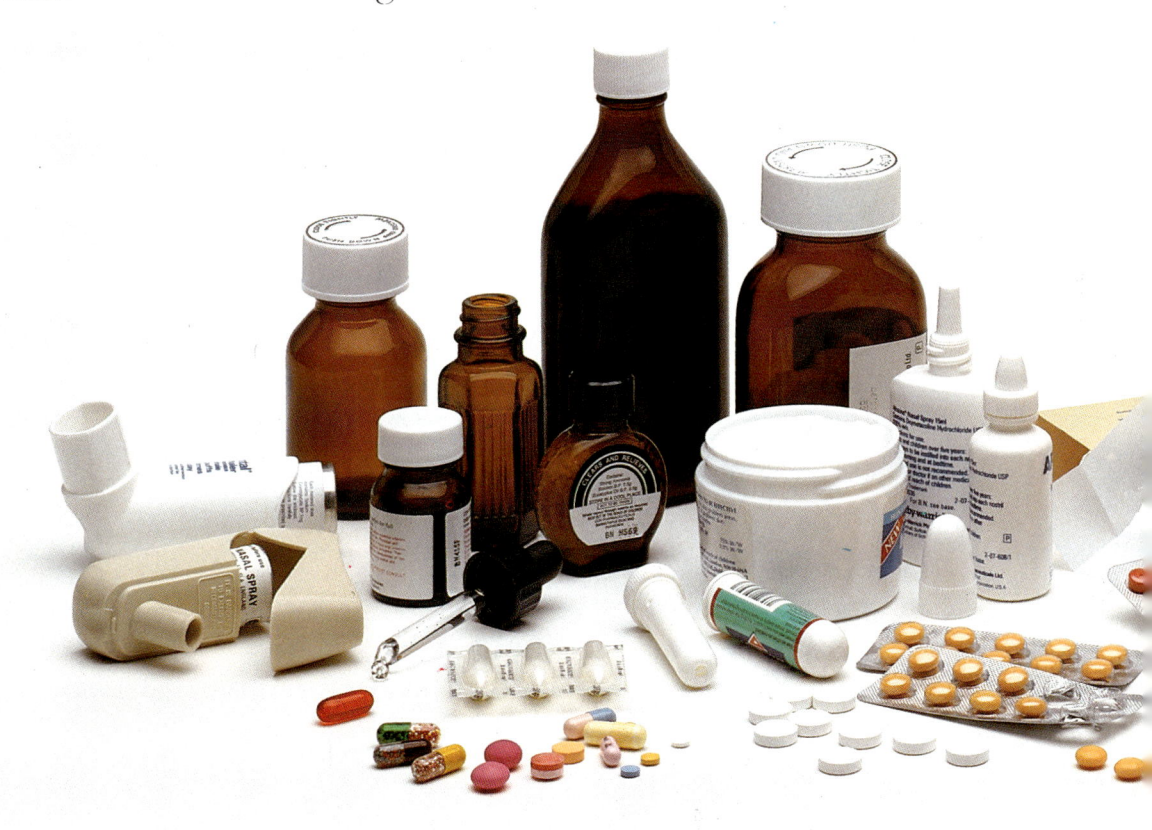

There are thousands of different types of medical drugs. They are designed to be used for treating particular diseases or disorders, but most are dangerous if misused. Tablets and capsules sold illegally on the street are often look-alike substitutes of unknown quality and content.

cause **addiction**, while others can produce unpleasant or dangerous effects when mixed with other drugs or with alcohol. Taking an overdose can, in some cases, cause death.

Among the medical drugs most likely to be abused are those which a doctor will prescribe to help a person relax, sleep better or cope with stress. Other medical drugs which may be abused are **stimulants**, intended to make a person feel more alert.

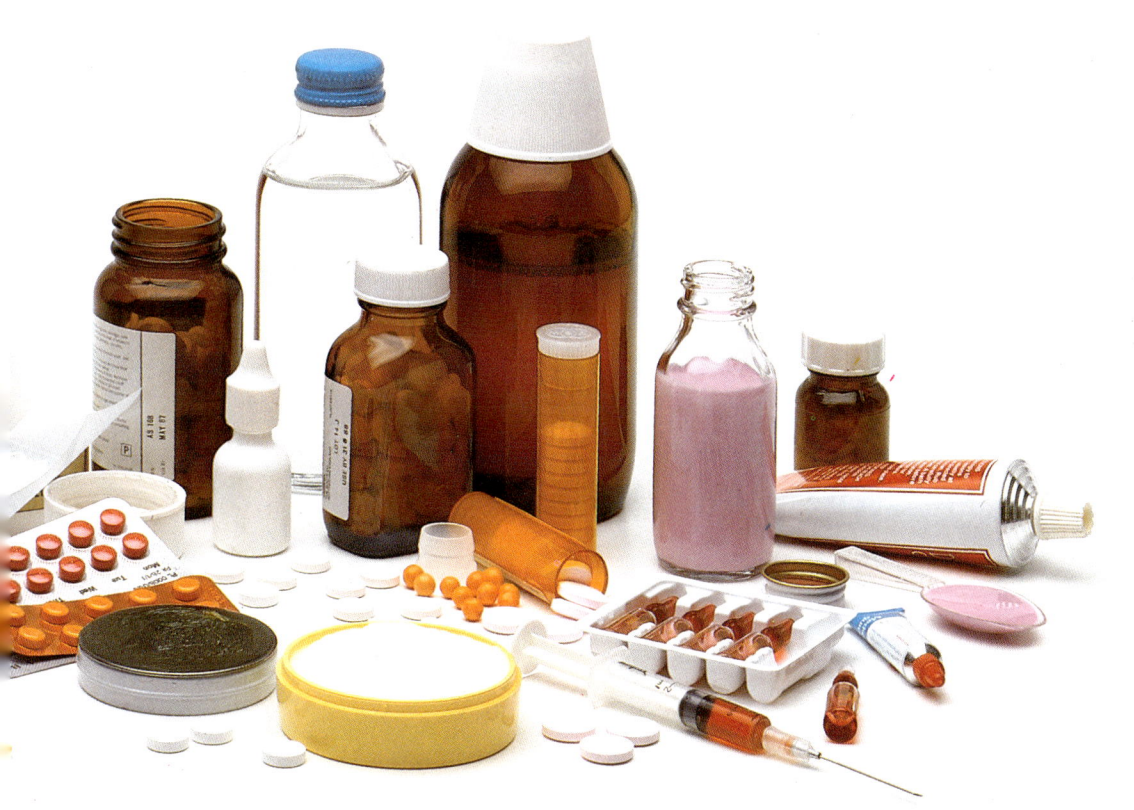

# Everyday drugs

Not all drugs are illegal. Many of us take them every day without thinking of them as "drugs" at all.

Alcohol is a drug which has a powerful effect on the brain; so is the **nicotine** in tobacco smoke. Both can produce addiction, just like the "hard" drugs such as heroin. Most people now understand that these everyday drugs can damage health, but they are still used in very large amounts.

Alcohol is a **depressant** drug. This means that it causes relaxation, and if taken in large amounts makes the drinker sleepy. But some users become addicted and cannot do without alcohol. They risk damage to the **liver** and to other organs.

The nicotine in cigarette smoke is carried in the blood to the brain. It also affects the heart and blood circulation, while the tar in cigarettes is known to be the main cause of **lung cancer**.

But we also take drugs which seem to be harmless. Tea, coffee and chocolate all contain **caffeine**, which is a powerful stimulant drug affecting the brain. We certainly don't experience a "high" after drinking coffee or tea, although we do feel more alert.

*Opposite*

Tobacco and alcohol are among the most common everyday drugs. Most people do not think of them as being "real" drugs, but they can still cause addiction. A substance is not necessarily harmless just because it is legal. All of the items in this picture are drugs that have an effect on both mind and body. The effects of caffeine, found in tea and coffee, are so mild that these "drugs" very rarely cause problems unless taken in very large quantities. Caffeine is also added to most cola drinks.

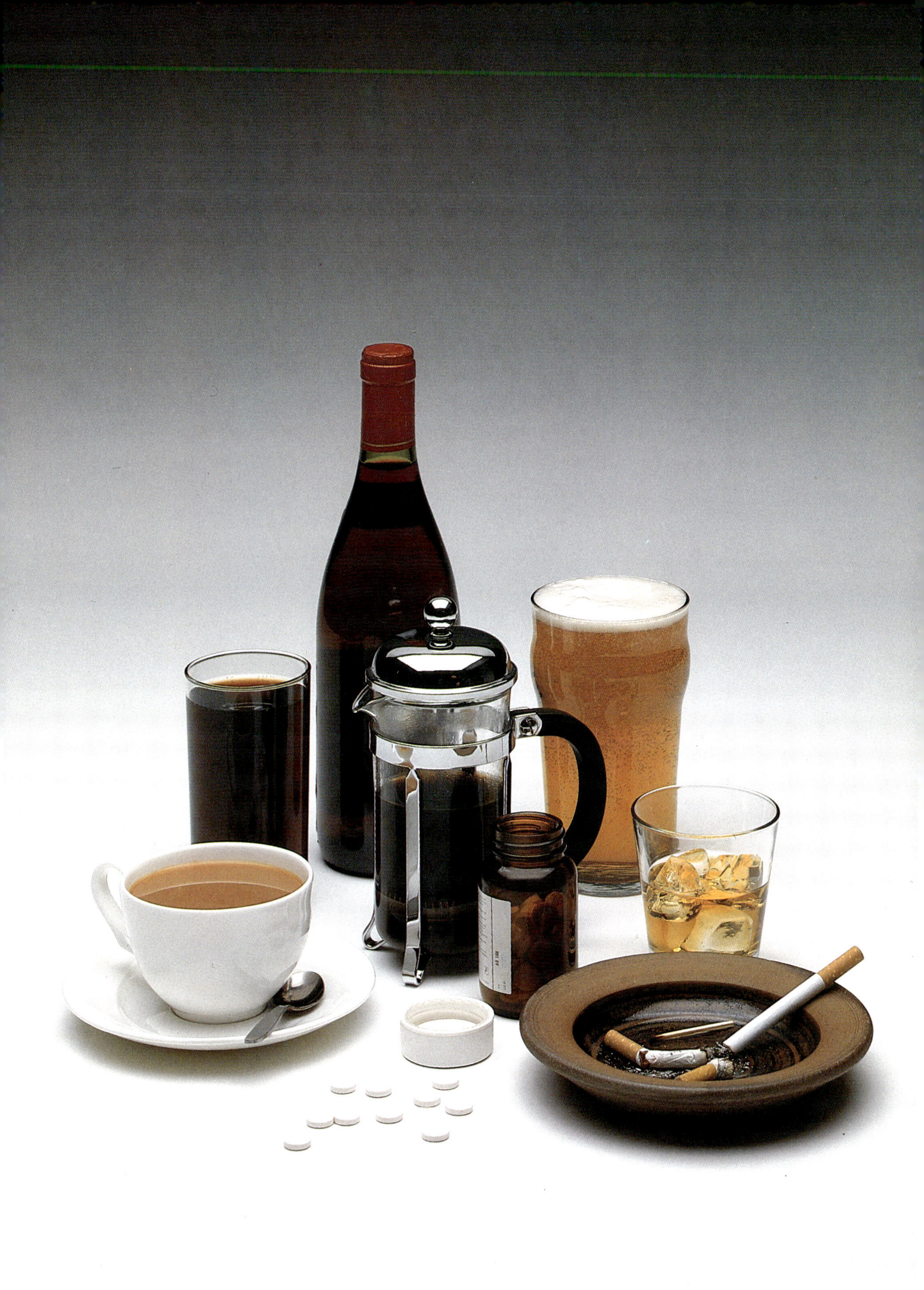

# Addiction

One of the risks of experimenting with drugs is that many of them are addictive, or cause **dependence**. This means that it becomes physically or emotionally uncomfortable or even impossible to do without the drug.

When an addictive drug is first taken, users describe the feeling as one of intense pleasure known as the "**high**". The user may take the drug again to repeat the experience. But after a time the user needs a larger dose of the drug to produce the same result, because the brain develops a **tolerance**, or becomes used to the drug. So the dose of the drug has to be increased, while the "satisfaction" decreases.

By now the drug has had a long-lasting or even a permanent effect on the brain. The user has become dependent upon the drug. Unless the drug is present in the blood at quite high levels, the user experiences **withdrawal symptoms**. These can be extremely unpleasant sensations like stomach cramps, pain and vomiting.

To avoid these withdrawal sensations, and to "feed" the habit, an addict has to keep taking the drug.

When a drug is taken for the first time, it takes only a small amount to produce a "high". But as the body gets used to the drug, it becomes more and more difficult to achieve the same effect, so the user needs to take greater amounts of the drug. In time the user may need to take the drug just to feel "normal".

**"High" (level of satisfaction)**

**Drug dose**

Addiction to a drug begins after it has been taken several times. With a powerful drug like crack addiction can begin almost from the first dose, although most drugs take longer. It is this uncertainty which makes experimentation so dangerous.

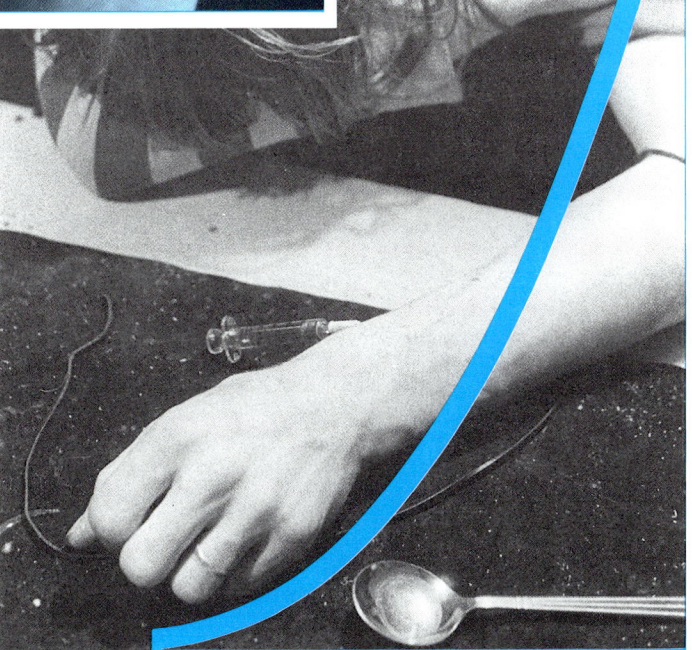

**Number of drug doses**

**Risk of addiction**

13

# The drug habit

The reasons for taking the first dose of a drug vary widely. Some people start to take drugs out of curiosity, without worrying about addiction. They think they can take a few doses without any risk. Others may experiment with drugs out of boredom, because they feel they have nothing better to do.

Many young people begin because they are introduced to drugs by friends. In any group of people there is always pressure to join in with the rest and not to be seen as an outsider. This "peer group pressure" can be difficult to resist. Older members of the group may suggest that it is more adult to take drugs, or that a newcomer must take drugs if he or she wants to belong.

For some people drugs can seem to offer an escape from the pressures that affect us all. Unemployment and boredom are believed to be important reasons why some young people start to take drugs and then continue with the habit. For others it is the thrill of taking risks, knowing that drug abuse is illegal. Drug taking is often a gesture of defiance against authority, against parents, or against society as a whole.

*Opposite*

Drugs are sold or "pushed" wherever groups of young people gather. If you think that drugs are being offered, it is safest to avoid the place completely. You run the risk of becoming involved in a drug raid, even if you are completely innocent.

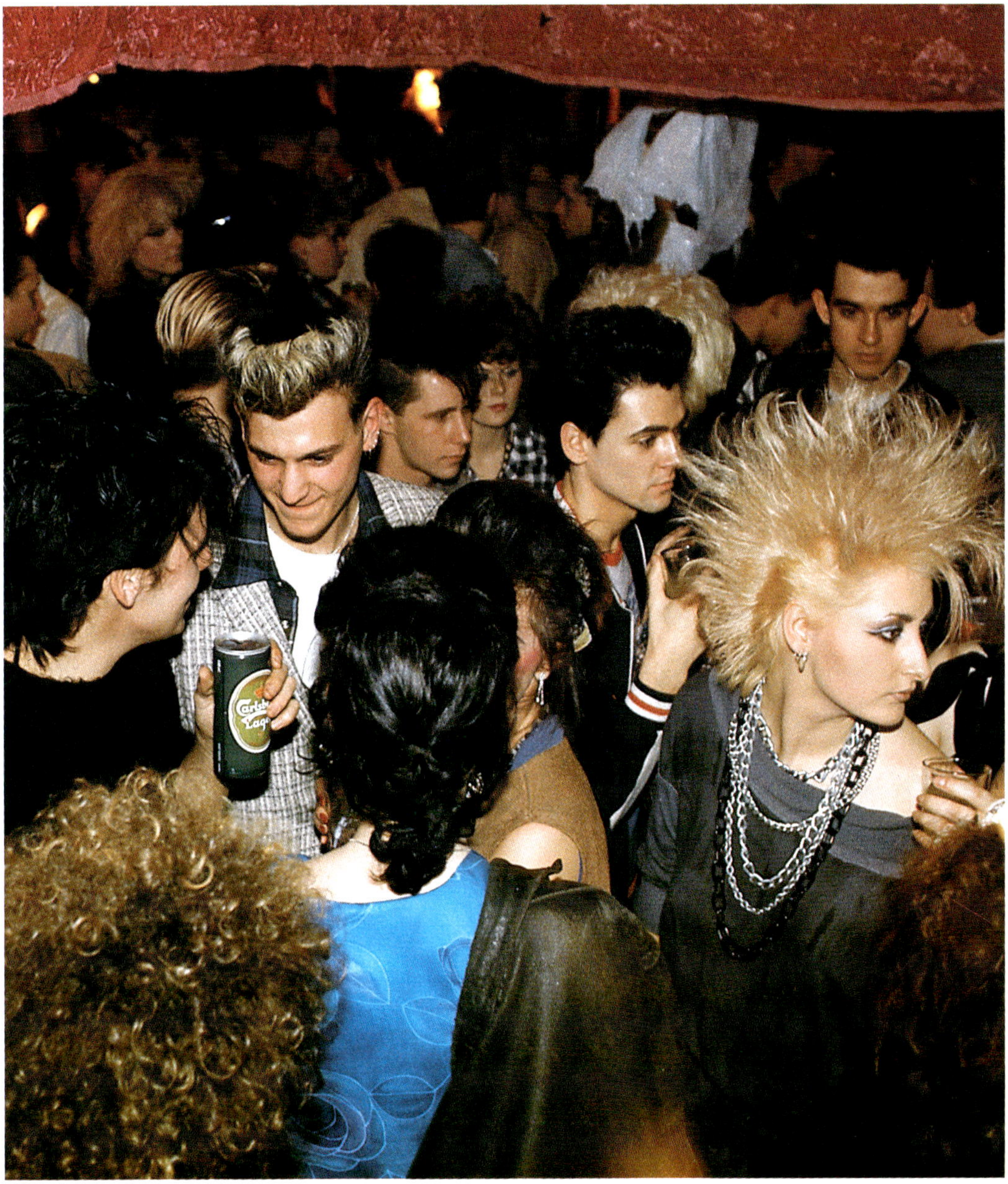

# The social effects of drug taking

The physical effects of drug taking can be very serious, but for many users the social effects are even worse.

Most drugs are either stimulants or depressants. This means that users are frequently excitable, irritable and aggressive, or else withdrawn and morose.

After starting with casual experimentation, and drifting into heavier usage, the regular user finds him or herself more and more cut off from "normal" life. Friends and family may be upset or annoyed at the unpredictable changes in behaviour. This in turn can encourage the user to depend more heavily on the drugs to insulate him or her from reality.

People who use and buy drugs illegally risk coming into conflict with the law. They have set themselves against what is usually considered "normal" behaviour. Taking such risks may be part of the appeal for some, but the stress and fear of being caught will eventually affect behaviour, family life and school work.

The high cost of drugs means that the drug user is often forced into crime to pay for further supplies.

*Opposite*
Drug users need large amounts of money to support their habit, and many are forced into crime in order to buy drugs. Users of "soft" drugs like cannabis may be offered "hard" drugs too, and may be tempted to take the next step which can lead to dependence.

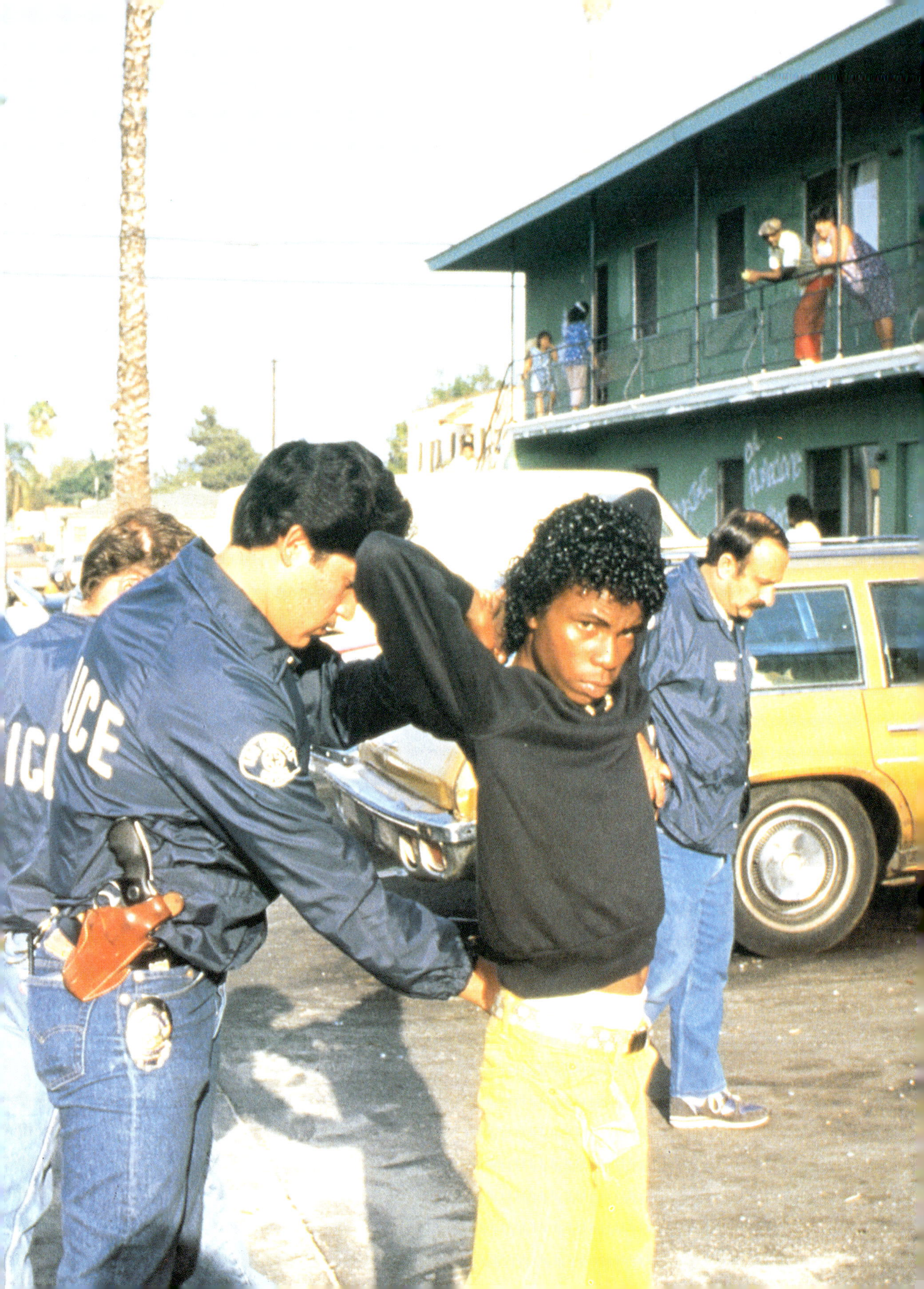

# Glues and solvents

Glue sniffing, or solvent abuse, is the most common form of drug taking, particularly among children. Certain types of glues and household products contain solvents which give off fumes. When breathed in, they produce a kind of intoxication, rather like drunkenness. Further sniffing causes giddiness, confusion and often aggressiveness. Sometimes sniffing produces **hallucinations** – visions or imaginary pictures that can cause panic.

Solvent sniffing is not truly addictive. It seems to run in brief fashions in a school or area, and most young people give it up after a period of experimentation. But for some it can become a dangerous habit.

The tell-tale marks of solvent abuse. Some try it out of curiosity or because their friends sniff glue. Others are simply seeking attention. Whatever the reasons, solvent abuse can cause serious problems and accidental death from choking or suffocation.

The risks are not so much from the solvents themselves, although large amounts probably do cause damage to the liver and lungs. Young people "high" on solvents can become involved in violence or have accidents, such as serious burns from inflammable glues. Some have suffocated as a result of using plastic bags to concentrate the fumes. Others have choked to death on their own vomit, having passed out while sniffing. Inhaling from aerosol cans is highly dangerous and has caused a number of deaths.

A wide range of household products contain solvents. The sale of glues and solvents to young people is controlled by law, but it is impossible to prevent all such substances from getting into the wrong hands.

# Cannabis

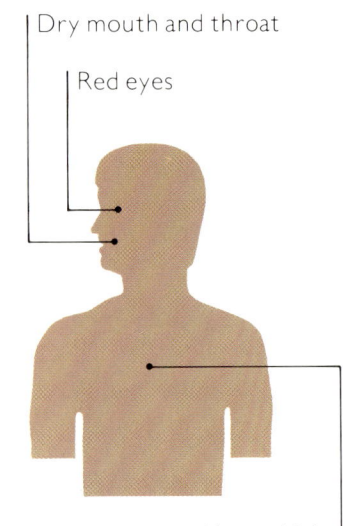

Dry mouth and throat

Red eyes

Lung cancer and bronchitis

Cannabis affects the brain, and smoking it may lead to chest problems such as **bronchitis** and lung cancer. Regular use is thought to damage short-term memory. Cannabis is not thought to be physically addictive, but it may produce psychological dependence.

Cannabis or marijuana (also known by many slang names) is a drug which affects the mind. It is obtained from the cannabis plant, which grows in warm climates. It is usually smoked, and produces a "high" in which the users become relaxed and giggly. Although they may feel that they have great insight and appreciation of colours, music and conversation, to onlookers they just appear mildly intoxicated. Continued use makes the user very sleepy.

It is doubtful if cannabis causes true physical addiction, but regular users can certainly develop an emotional dependence and find it difficult to do without the drug.

After smoking cannabis, the pulse rate increases, eyes become bloodshot, and the mouth and throat become dry. Cannabis also affects concentration and coordination, making it dangerous (and illegal) to drive while under its influence. In some people it can cause panic attacks, and in very heavy users, it may cause "burn out", a condition in which the user becomes dulled and sluggish. It is suspected that heavy cannabis smokers also risk lung cancer.

◁ Cannabis grows best in fairly hot, dry climates. It is cultivated in very large amounts in Central America and the Middle and Far East, and then smuggled into other countries.

▷ Cannabis is sold in many forms. The most common is "grass" or herbal cannabis. This is the dried leaves and flowers of the plant. It is mixed with tobacco, rolled into "joints" and smoked. Another, more concentrated form is cannabis resin.

# Cocaine

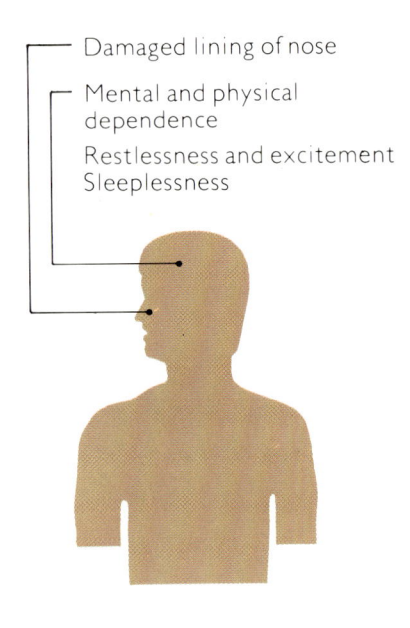

- Damaged lining of nose
- Mental and physical dependence
- Restlessness and excitement
- Sleeplessness

Cocaine is a stimulant which produces very strong psychological dependence, more difficult to overcome than physical addiction. It may be physically addictive too. When sniffed or injected, it produces a feeling of alertness and well being, but it can also cause anxiety and panic, eventually leading to mental illness. Continued use damages the lining of the nose.

For many years, the use of cocaine was limited by its very high price. It was sometimes known as the "rich man's drug". Because of this it was usually "cut" or mixed with cheaper substances. But now cocaine is being smuggled in huge quantities by organized crime groups. As a result, the price of cocaine has dropped dramatically, and its use is becoming a growing problem. In the United States alone, it is thought that 5 million people use cocaine regularly, and another 5,000 try the drug for the first time every day.

Cocaine is a powerful stimulant. It is a white powder, usually sniffed, or "snorted", up the nose, from where it is quickly absorbed into the blood. It produces an almost immediate "high" which makes the user feel excited and confident. The effect wears off quickly, and gives way to irritability and anxiety. It is impossible to sleep while under the effects of the drug, so the user becomes very tired and depressed, needing more and more of the drug to obtain the stimulant effect. The cocaine habit can quickly become very expensive to maintain.

For centuries the coca leaf has been chewed by South American Indians to suppress hunger and tiredness. The leaf contains small amounts of cocaine. South America is the main area where the drug is produced illegally.

**Cocaine-growing areas**

Cocaine dealers measure out the powder for sale on the street. Because the drug is still quite expensive, it is sometimes "cut" by mixing it with other substances. There is no way of knowing how strong the powder is.

# Crack: a new threat

Until quite recently it was believed that cocaine was not truly addictive: that its use was just a habit that was easy to break. But now a new and much more dangerous form of the drug has appeared in the United States and it is already spreading to other parts of the world.

Crack is a form of cocaine which has been chemically treated to produce large white crystals. The drug is taken by smoking it, known as "freebasing". Because it is almost pure cocaine, it produces a very powerful high, together with an almost uncontrollable craving for the drug, sometimes after only one or two doses.

Because of its strength, there is an even greater risk of overdosing when using crack. Deaths from overdoses of crack are becoming common in areas where the drug is easily available. As with most other drugs, "look alikes" are often sold to unsuspecting users. These and other substances used to cut the drug can also be dangerous to health.

Babies born to mothers who have taken crack have shown withdrawal symptoms straight away. Many have died as a result of their mother's addiction.

*Opposite*

Crack is a very concentrated form of cocaine which has only recently appeared. The drug is made into large brittle chunks, which are broken up and smoked or "freebased".

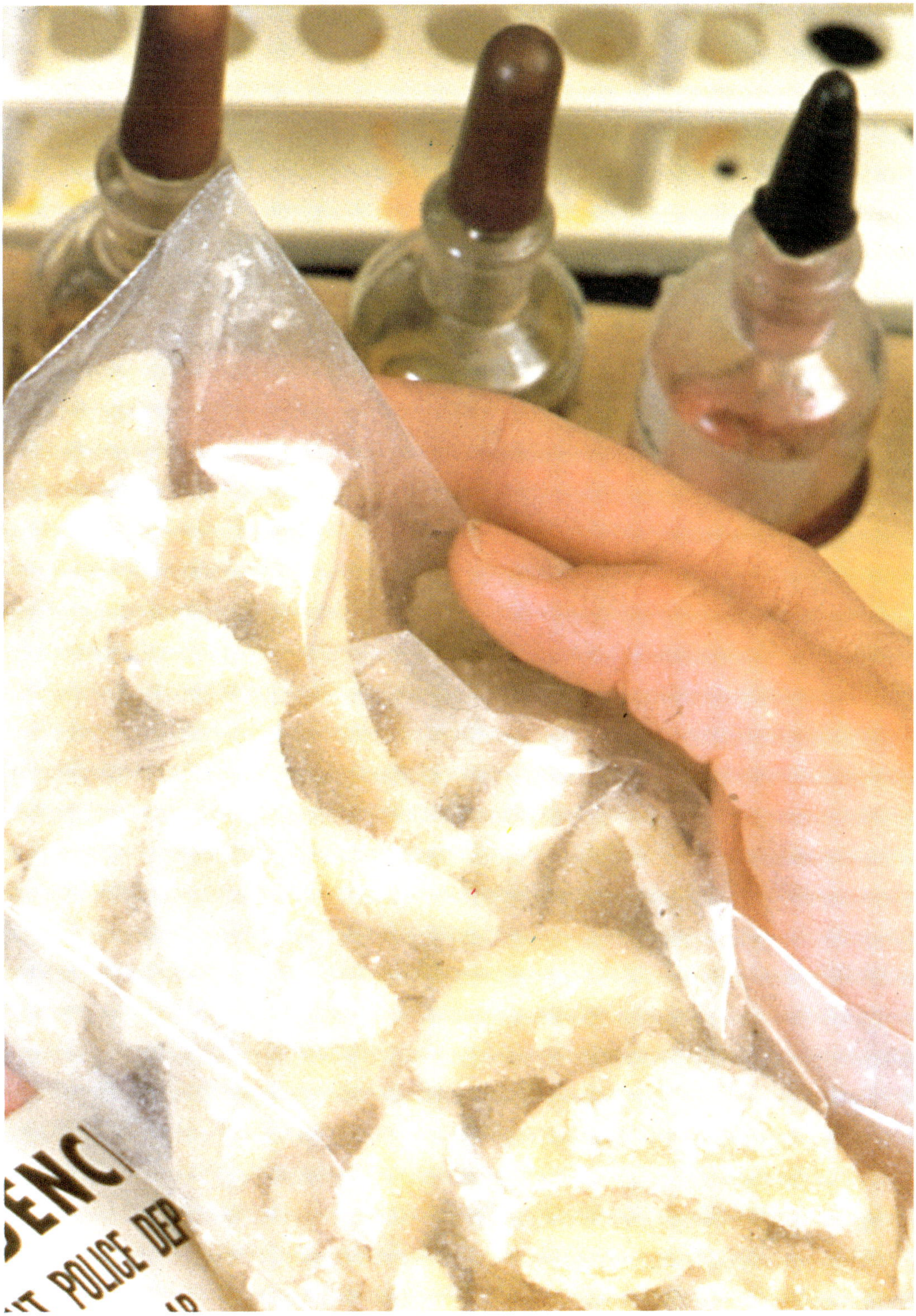

# Heroin

Heroin is the most widely known of the addictive **narcotic** drugs. Like others of this type of drug, it was first introduced as a medical drug, and is still sometimes used, under strict supervision, for relieving severe pain. It was first developed in the last century, as a painkiller which was not thought to be as strongly addictive as the related drug morphine. But heroin has proved to cause even stronger addiction.

Heroin and morphine are produced from the raw drug opium, which is itself obtained from the oriental poppy. Opium and the drugs produced from it are smuggled to other countries, where most of it is converted into heroin.

The opium poppy from which heroin is produced is grown in two main areas in Asia. The Golden Crescent extends from Pakistan, across Afghanistan and Iran, into Turkey. The Golden Triangle is an area between Thailand, Laos, and Burma.

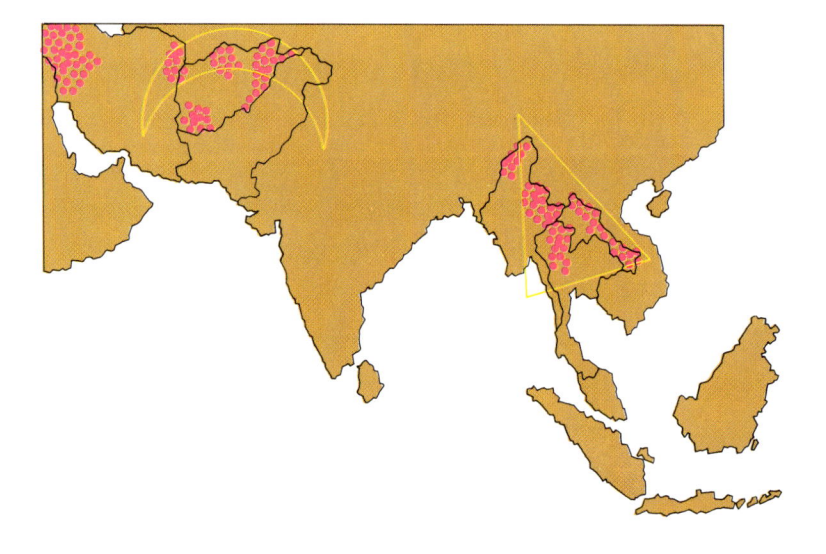

In its pure form heroin is a white powder, but it is almost always mixed or "cut" with other substances before being sold on the street.

Until recently most heroin users injected the drug into a vein ("mainlining") or under the skin ("skin popping"). But users may also inhale the fumes of heated heroin (known as "chasing the dragon"). This habit is just as strongly addictive as injection.

Poppy heads are scored with a special knife. The opium which oozes out is collected and smuggled abroad for processing into heroin.

# The effects of heroin

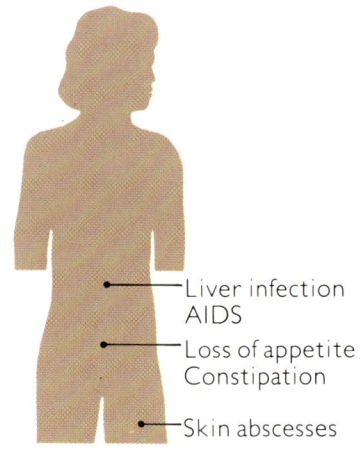

Liver infection
AIDS
Loss of appetite
Constipation
Skin abscesses

Heroin and related drugs cause strong physical and emotional dependence. They cause sedation, and produce physical effects such as constipation, slowed breathing and heart rate.

Repeated injection into a vein, using a dirty needle causes **abscesses**. Eventually the vein collapses and can no longer be used. The user keeps moving to undamaged areas in an attempt to inject the drug, leaving tell-tale **track marks**. Drug users who share needles also risk catching AIDS.

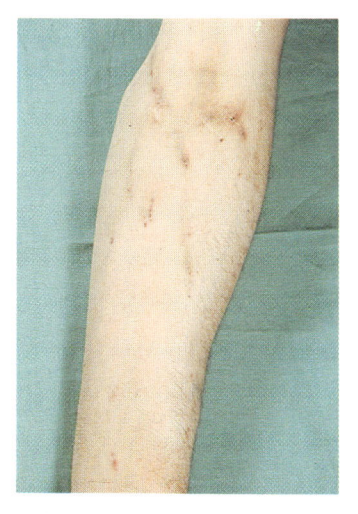

However heroin is taken, it at first produces a powerful "high". This initial feeling is followed by relaxation and a sense of relief from all stresses and worries.

But it takes larger and larger doses of the drug to reach the same "high", because the body soon develops a tolerance to the drug until, eventually, there is no pleasure in the habit. Instead, the user takes heroin just to prevent the onset of withdrawal symptoms. These are extremely unpleasant, both mentally and physically. The former user experiences anxiety, sleeplessness, desperation, and a terrible craving for the drug. Heroin is very strongly addictive, although the number of doses it takes to become addicted varies.

Besides having a powerful effect on the mind, heroin causes constipation and loss of appetite. Even worse effects may be caused by the materials with which the drug is mixed, or "cut". These can cause infections which damage the veins. Addicts who inject often share needles, and they run the risk of catching infections like hepatitis, as well as the more serious threat of **AIDS**.

Two registered heroin addicts collect a day's supply from a clinic in Italy. In some countries, drugs such as heroin or a substitute drug are given under medical supervision to reduce withdrawal effects while addicts are being treated. This means that they will not be using dangerously impure "street" drugs, and do not have to resort to crime for the money to buy drugs.

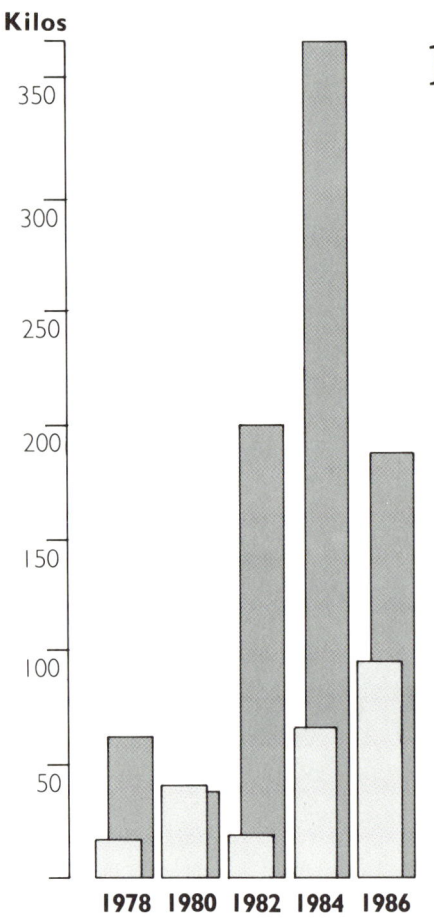

# Drugs and organized crime

Drug smuggling is very big business and it is truly international. Because huge profits are involved, drug supply has become part of organized crime with international connections. Although there may be only a few key people at the top organizing the drug trade, a large number of lesser criminals are involved in the smuggling and distribution of drugs. At street level millions of people act as drug dealers. Many of these are addicts themselves, raising money for their next "fix". Because so many people are involved, it is very difficult to control or stamp out the drug trade unless the organizers can be caught.

Drug seizures by UK Customs over several years show the changing pattern of drug fashion. Cocaine is now beginning to catch up with heroin as the most widespread "hard" drug.

▷ Customs officials are skilled at spotting drug smugglers, and at identifying drugs being smuggled in bulk. Even so, only a small proportion of drugs are intercepted by police and customs, and the supply is never shut off.

The drugs which are smuggled are mainly those produced from plants, such as cannabis, heroin and cocaine. Cannabis is bulky, so it is less easy to conceal than concentrated drugs like heroin and cocaine. Heroin is processed from opium somewhere along the route from the Asian countries where the poppy is grown. The concentrated drug is carried by smugglers from the processing laboratories, which are often in the Mediterranean countries. The cocaine business, too, has produced a large and violent underworld throughout the Caribbean and southern United States.

At every stage in the chain of supply, very large profits are made. It is the middlemen, drug smugglers, drug processors and dealers who profit. For the farmer, coca, opium or cannabis is just another crop.

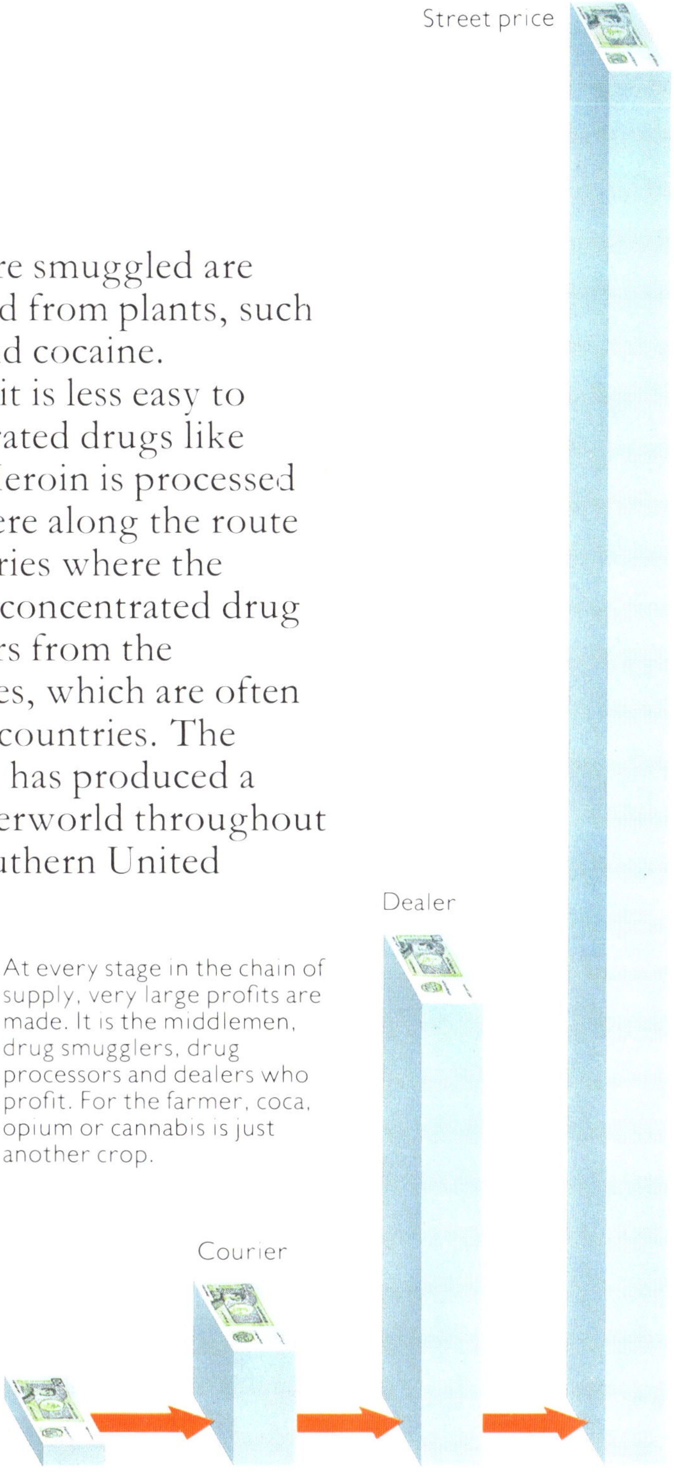

Farmer → Courier → Dealer → Street price

# Tranquillizers

Like heroin, tranquillizers were developed for proper medical purposes. But unlike that drug, they are still very widely used and frequently prescribed by doctors. Tranquillizers are given to help calm anxiety and agitation when these become a medical problem.

Tranquillizers calm the user down, but they also produce a pleasant relaxed feeling in people who are *not* anxious at all. They can make people feel carefree and slightly drunk.

It has only recently been realized that tranquillizers are capable of producing addiction, similar to but less serious than that caused by heroin and other "hard" drugs. Sudden withdrawal can cause wakefulness, anxiety, sickness and other more serious problems.

People who have had tranquillizers legally prescribed in large doses over several years can become dependent on them. This often makes it difficult for the doctor to reduce the dose and "wean" the addict off the drug. Tranquillizers are not made illegally, as they are so readily available, but are sometimes stolen or obtained from people having legal prescriptions.

*Opposite*
The stresses of modern living cause tension and anxiety which are often "treated" with tranquillizers. But overuse of these drugs has recently been found to cause problems of addiction.

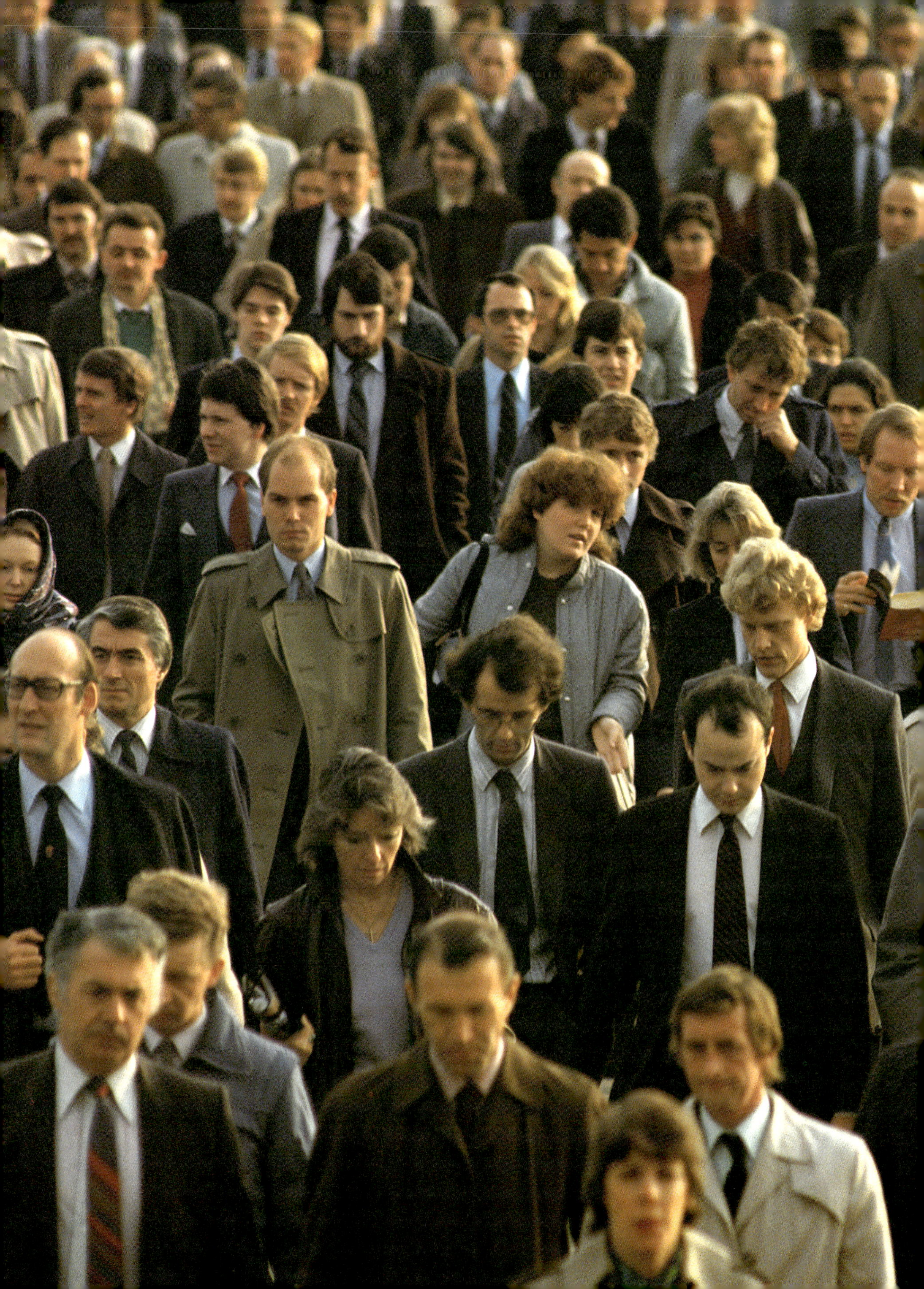

# Uppers and downers

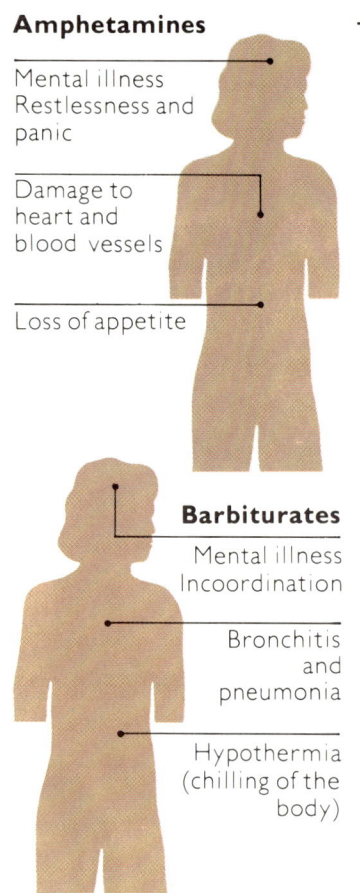

**Amphetamines**
- Mental illness / Restlessness and panic
- Damage to heart and blood vessels
- Loss of appetite

**Barbiturates**
- Mental illness / Incoordination
- Bronchitis and pneumonia
- Hypothermia (chilling of the body)

Amphetamines are powerful stimulants which make the user feel full of energy and confidence. They can cause very strong emotional dependence. Regular use can cause mental illness and reduce resistance to disease. Barbiturates make the user very tired and subdued. They can cause lasting physical and mental damage.

*Opposite*

For many years, barbiturate drugs and other sedatives were prescribed to help people sleep. Doctors are now aware of the dangers of these drugs, but many elderly people are still addicted to them.

Amphetamines and barbiturates are both medical drugs. Their effects are roughly opposite. Amphetamines ("uppers") are stimulants, while barbiturates ("downers") are depressants. Both have been used very widely in the past, but doctors now realize that they can have very unpleasant side effects, and may be misused by addicts. Because they are cheap and readily available, they represent a major drug problem.

Amphetamines produce a very powerful high, which users call the "rush". The user feels very alert and full of energy, but will be unable to sleep. To the onlooker, however, the user seems aggressive, excited and confused. When the effects wear off, the user becomes depressed and irritable. Heavy users may become psychologically addicted and can suffer mental illness.

Barbiturates are very dangerous drugs which produce a dreamy relaxed state. They are very powerfully addictive, and sudden withdrawal can cause convulsions or even death. Barbiturate drugs can interfere with breathing, especially when taken with alcohol. This combination kills many users every year.

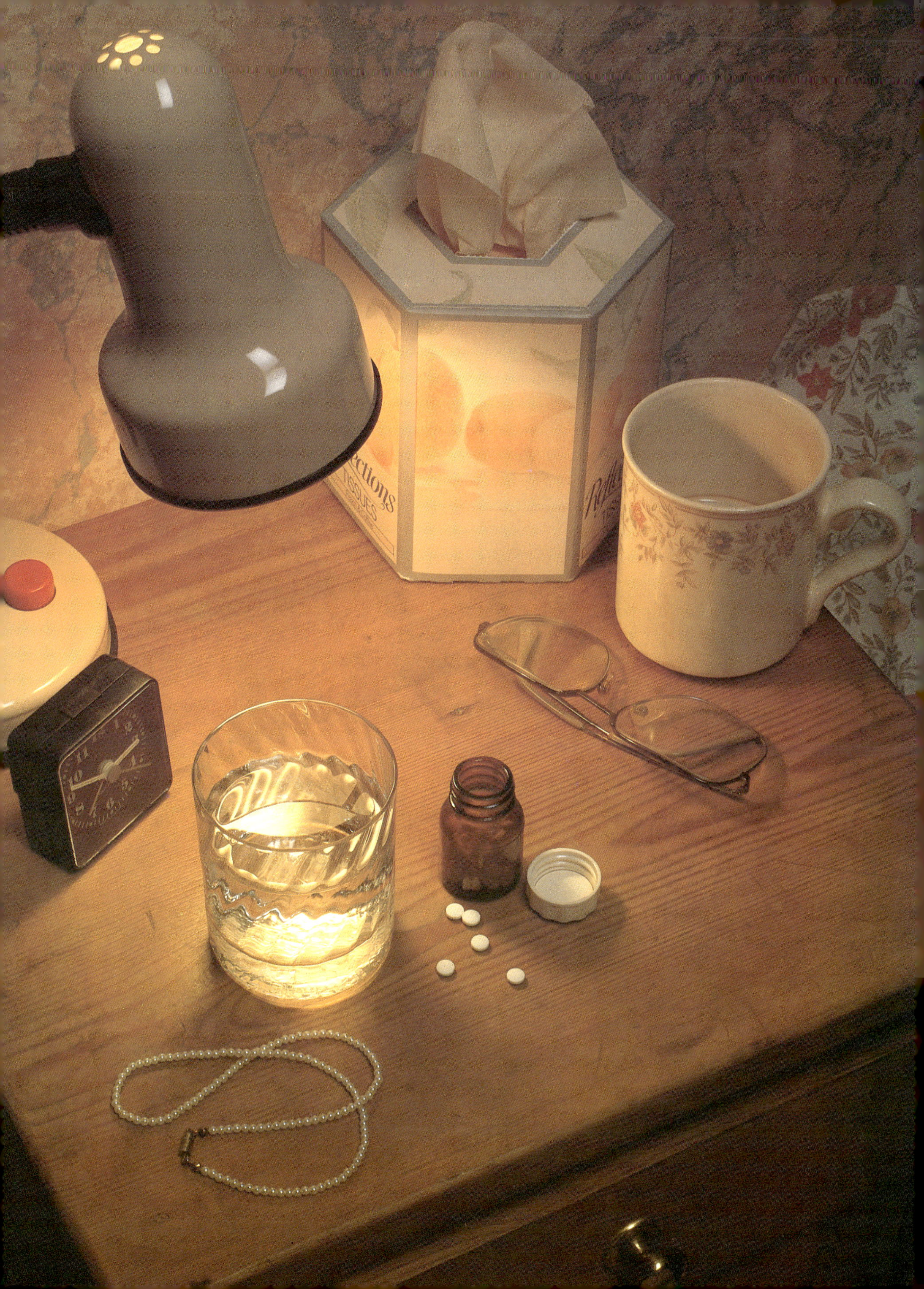
TISSUES

# LSD

LSD, or acid, is one of the most potent drugs known. It has extremely powerful effects on the brain in almost unimaginably small doses.

It is always swallowed, sometimes on a sugar lump, or as very small tablets, or as a tiny speck on a piece of paper. It produces a peculiar mental state called a **trip**, in which the user experiences hallucinations. These can be very beautiful, or extremely frightening, but the effects are unpredictable, even when the same person repeats the experience.

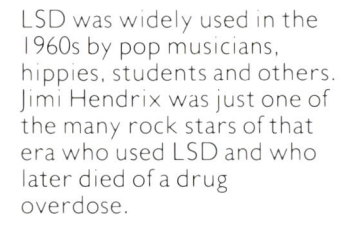

LSD was widely used in the 1960s by pop musicians, hippies, students and others. Jimi Hendrix was just one of the many rock stars of that era who used LSD and who later died of a drug overdose.

"LSD can take you to places you never dreamed of" runs the caption to this poster which stresses the risks of mental illness. A "bad trip" on LSD can be a terrifying experience which can occur again without taking further doses of the drug.

For some, the trip may be repeated, even weeks or months after taking LSD, and a few users have long attacks resembling mental illness.

LSD does not produce physical addiction, but it does have risks. Some users panic while on a "bad trip" and may injure themselves. Others may become involved in accidents or become violent because their sense of reality is distorted by the drug.

# Drugs outside the law

Drug users often try to get around the laws controlling drugs by finding sources which are not illegal. There are many natural sources of drugs, but most of these are as dangerous as the illegal ones. Some toadstools, for example, contain drug-like substances, but many are very poisonous. It is *extremely* dangerous to experiment, for the effects are unpredictable.

This is also the case with synthetic drugs, such as PCP, or "Angel Dust". It creates a feeling of being separated from the body, but may also cause attacks of panic.

The common Fly Agaric contains a drug-like substance, but it tastes very unpleasant, causes violent vomiting and is poisonous.

The Peyote cactus of Mexico and the United States contains a drug resembling LSD. It is still taken by some American Indians in religious ceremonies.

Tiny Liberty Caps contain a drug similar to LSD. They are very difficult to distinguish from similar fungi which taste unpleasant or may be poisonous.

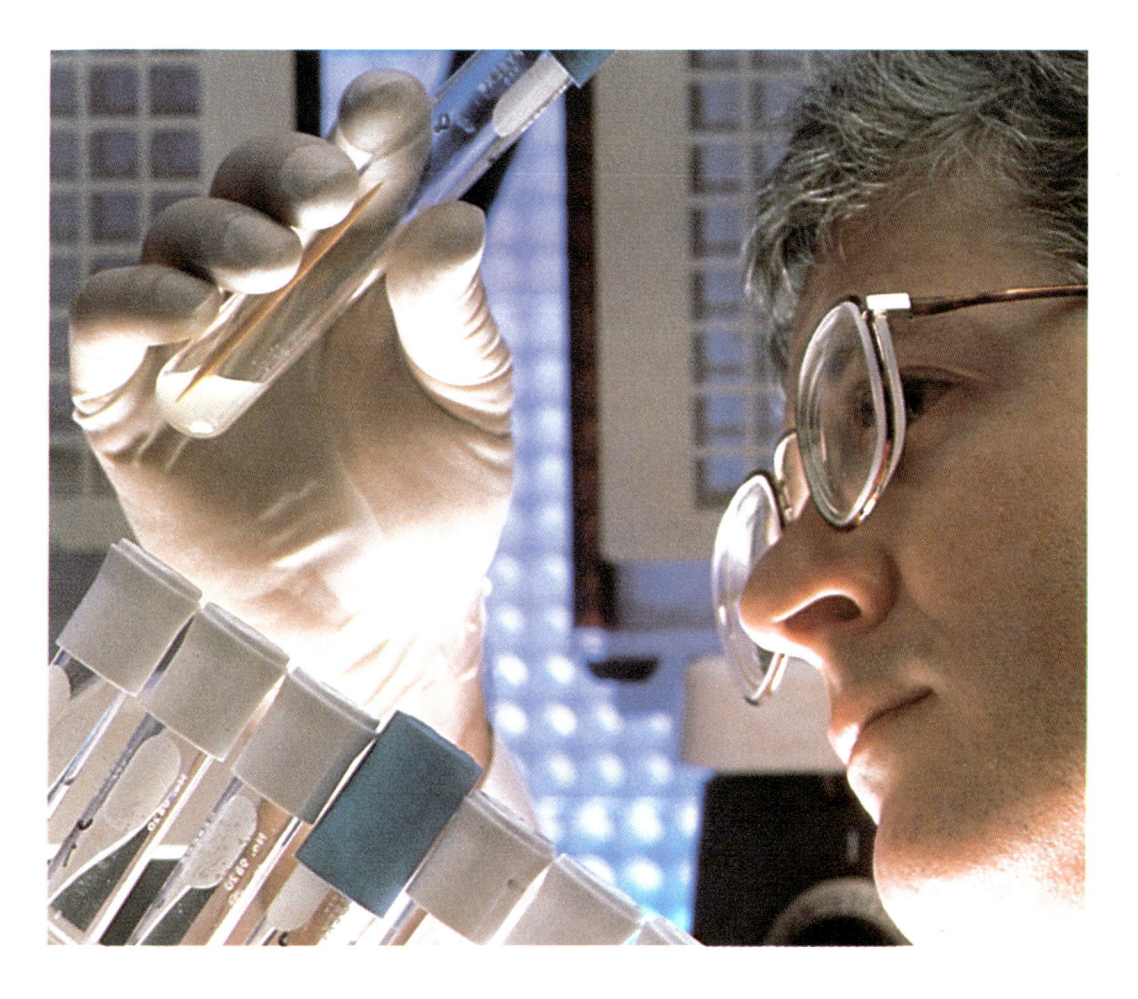

"Designer drugs" are a new development. Chemists working illegally in laboratories make slight alterations to an existing drug so that it is no longer covered by current drug laws. The effects of the drug can also be altered. In California, for example, 20 percent of the state's 200,000 heroin addicts use synthetic drugs. Some of these are up to 40 times stronger than heroin, while one type is *800* times as strong! And another type of designer drug was recently found to cause permanent brain damage.

"Designer drugs" are often produced in quite simple laboratories, so their manufacture is difficult to control. Such laboratories do not have proper facilities to test the quality of the drugs they produce, and many people have been poisoned by their use.

# Recognizing a drug problem

**Common signs of a drug problem**

- Sudden mood changes – becoming depressed and sullen.
- Irritable behaviour.
- Loss of appetite.
- Loss of interest in hobbies and sports.
- Secretive behaviour.
- Petty theft.
- Unusual smells or stains on clothing. Marks on arms, legs or lips.
- Unusual tablets, powder, or scorched metal foil.
- Unusual restlessness or sleepiness.

What are the warning signs that someone may be getting involved with drugs? And how can you be sure that they are really using drugs, not just bragging?

Although drug abuse is a very serious problem, it is important to remember that most young people *don't* take drugs. Those that do experiment usually take them only once or twice out of curiosity. Others are pressured into taking drugs by friends, or try them because they are bored or depressed. Only a few will become regular users, but for some, drug-taking will become a habit that affects health and can even threaten life.

It is very difficult to tell if someone uses drugs occasionally, unless you see them doing it. In really heavy users, the signs of bad health are usually obvious. But for those who are just beginning to develop a real problem, it is important to spot the warning signs in time to do something about it.

Most of the warning signs depend on a change of behaviour. Don't jump to hasty conclusions – many of these signs are quite normal in young people, but when many occur together, they suggest that a drug problem may be developing.

Unexpected and uncharacteristic changes of mood can sometimes be a sign of a drug problem. These are usually only obvious in a person you know very well.

Sedative drugs cause drowsiness, but even after taking stimulants, a drug user will eventually become drowsy. A person who becomes very sleepy after taking drugs may be suffering from an overdose. They need urgent medical treatment.

The use of solvents or amphetamines can cause a person to become aggressive, as can mixtures of other drugs.

Heroin, amphetamines and some other drugs cause loss of appetite. If a person is a heavy user of any drug, they may be on a continual "high" where they can't be bothered to eat.

# What to do if a friend is taking drugs

There is no special sort of person who takes drugs, or who would never take them. Drugs are obtainable everywhere, and people from all types of backgrounds are at risk.

The first thing to do if you think a friend may have a drug problem is to raise the subject with them and talk it over. This may be embarrassing, but if you know him or her well enough you can risk it. After all, it's for your friend's benefit.

If you are uncertain about the situation, or feel that you can't talk to your friend directly, you will need to get help from someone else. This does *not* mean getting your friend into trouble by accusing them of taking drugs. You will have to find the right person to talk to, who will help without making matters worse.

There are drug advice centres in most areas, and some will give help over the telephone. Advice and counselling centres understand the problems that can lead to drug dependence, and they are experts in helping young people. They give confidential advice on all aspects of drug dependence and its treatment.

*Opposite*

Former drug users need a lot of support if they are not to resume their habit. Drug counsellors offer understanding and advice when the craving for drugs becomes too strong. Some addicts need help for many months until they are able to cope unaided.

Eastend
Kathy
steps in
Valerie
takes on
key task
Access to
prisoners
AA Greater
London
Street
Atlas
Greater London Street Atlas

# Getting off drugs

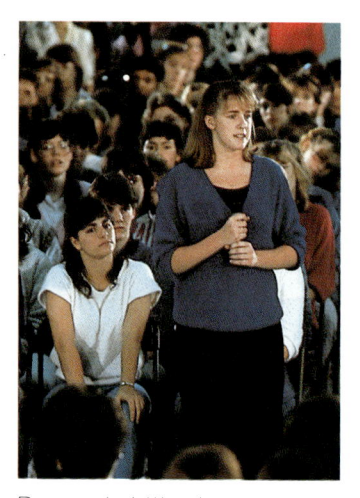

Drug rehabilitation centres give help and support to drug users who want to give up the habit. This American centre, near Washington D.C., was visited by the Princess of Wales and Nancy Reagan in 1985, both of whom have given their support to anti-drugs campaigns.

When a drug user has made the decision to stop, and actually *wants* to give up drugs, he or she has gone a long way towards breaking the habit. With drugs like cannabis or solvents it may be easy to stop. But for "hard" drugs like heroin or cocaine, where there is a strong physical or psychological addiction, proper treatment will be needed, together with a long period of support and encouragement.

Withdrawal from drug addiction is usually short and sharp, although the symptoms are very unpleasant. It is the aftereffects which are hard to live with while the craving for drugs is still strong. Mixing with friends who still take drugs provides too great a temptation, so this means making a clean break from the drug-using group.

There are many clinics and therapy groups which can help drug users to break their habits, and with medical help, to stay off drugs. These groups encourage users explain their feelings and their problems, without blaming them for having become involved with drugs. They also help former users resume a normal life.

To help fight the drug problem, pop personalities such as Pete Townshend, a former drug user, have given their support to health-education campaigns.

Former users need a lot of love and support from their real, non-drug-using friends and family while they go through this difficult time. For those who think they can never make the break, just remember how many people manage to give up smoking. Then consider: some doctors believe that smoking produces addiction even stronger than heroin.

# Glossary

**Abscess**: inflamed area of infection which is swollen with pus. An abscess is often caused by injecting drugs with a dirty needle.

**Addiction**: condition in which a drug user becomes unable to do without regular doses of a drug. The condition only develops after the drug has been taken several times.

**AIDS**: the abbreviation for "acquired immuno-deficiency syndrome". A growing health threat, this disease can be spread by injecting drugs with a needle previously used by an infected person. It is also spread by sexual activity.

**Bronchitis**: infection and inflammation of the bronchii, the tubes which carry air into the lungs. Smoking tobacco or drugs increases the risk of bronchitis.

**Caffeine**: a stimulant drug present in coffee, tea and other drinks, which increases the activity of the brain. It may cause restlessness and wakefulness if taken in large amounts.

**Dependence, physical**: form of addiction in which unpleasant physical effects are experienced when the drug is not available. These may include nausea, vomiting, aches and pains.

**Dependence, psychological (or emotional)**: form of addiction in which there is a very strong craving for the sensations that a drug produces.

**Depressant**: a drug which reduces the activity of the brain. This usually causes drowsiness and relaxation.

**Hallucination**: condition in which a drug user (or sometimes, a person suffering from an illness) experiences events which are not real. Most hallucinations are either "seen" or "heard"

**High**: the experience of being intoxicated after using a drug.

**Liver**: large organ in the abdomen, which among its other important functions, serves to break down drugs in the bloodstream and make them less harmful.

**Lung cancer**: common and very dangerous form of cancer among cigarette smokers. It is thought that cannabis smoking is also likely to cause lung cancer.

**Narcotic**: drug derived from opium, or one with a similar chemical structure. Common narcotic drugs include morphine, heroin and methadone.

# Where to go for help

**Nicotine**: stimulant drug found in tobacco. Nicotine causes the powerful addiction experienced by many smokers.

**Stimulant**: a drug which increases brain activity. It improves alertness in small doses.

**Tolerance**: condition in which the body adapts to the effects of a drug. This means that larger doses have to be taken to produce the same effects.

**Track marks**: line of scars, abscesses and other marks along a vein used to inject drugs. As the vein becomes damaged, the drug user is forced to move along to another healthy section in order to inject the drug, and eventually a "track" is formed.

**Trip**: drug intoxication, usually with a drug like LSD or "Magic Mushrooms".

**Withdrawal symptoms**: the unpleasant physical and emotional effects felt by an addict when a drug is not available.

There are many sources of information about drug problems. Most organizations providing help and advice will discuss problems over the telephone. Your local library may also be able to tell you about services in your area. Always remember that drugs are a medical problem and your family doctor will be able to give help and advice in confidence.

**Freephone Drug Problems**
Dial 100 and ask the operator for Freephone Drug Problems. A recorded message gives telephone numbers for contacts in areas throughout England.

In Scotland ring:
Scottish Drugs Forum
041 – 221 1175

In Wales ring:
All Wales Drugsline
0222 383313

In Northern Ireland ring:
0232 229808

If you cannot find a local service, write to:
**SCODA** (The Standing Conference on Drug Abuse)
1–4 Hatton Place
Hatton Garden
London EC1N 8ND
01 – 430 2341

**Families Anonymous**
88 Caledonian Road
London N1
01 – 278 8805
Advice and support for families
and friends of drug users.

**Release**
169 Commercial Street
London E1
01 – 603 8654 (emergency number).
Advise on legal problems connected with drug abuse.

**Australia and New Zealand**
Information and counselling services are available in most state capitals and regional centres. Contact these through the telephone directory or the operator.

47

# Index

abscess 28, 46
acid see LSD
addiction 6, 12–13, 14, 18, 20, 22, 24, 26, 27, 28, 32, 34, 37, 44, 46,
  see also dependence
advice centres 42, 47
AIDS 28, 46
alcohol 9, 10, 34
amphetamines 34, 41
"Angel Dust" 38
anti-drug campaign 7, 44, 45

barbiturates 34
behaviour changes 16, 40, 41
bronchitis 20, 46

caffeine 10, 46
cannabis 16–17, 31, 44
cigarettes 10
cocaine 22–3, 24, 25, 30, 31, 44
crack 13, 24, 25
customs seizures 30

deaths 18, 19, 24, 34
dependence 6, 7, 12, 13, 16, 42, 46
  physical 7, 22, 32, 46
  psychological 21, 22, 34, 46
depressant 10, 16, 34, 46
"designer drugs" 39
"downers" see barbiturates
drug advice centres 42, 47
drug dealing 23, 30, 31
drug seizures 30
drug smuggling 21, 22, 26, 27, 30, 31
drugs and the law 6, 8, 14, 16, 19, 20, 30, 38, 39

glue sniffing see solvent abuse
Golden Crescent 26
Golden Triangle 26
"grass" 21

hallucinations 18, 36, 46
hepatitis 28
heroin 26–7, 28–9, 30, 31, 32, 39, 41, 44, 45
"high" 12, 13, 19, 20, 22, 24, 28, 34, 41, 46

inhalants see solvent abuse
injection 22, 27, 28

joint 21

laboratory 31, 39
Liberty Cap 38
liver 10, 19, 46
LSD 36–7, 38
lung cancer 10, 20, 46

marijuana see cannabis
medical drugs 8–9, 26, 32
mental illness 22, 34, 37
morphine 26

narcotic 26, 46
nicotine 10, 47

opium 26, 27, 31
organized crime 22, 30, 31
overdose 9, 24, 36, 41

PCP 38
Peyote cactus 38

"rush" see high

solvent abuse 18–19, 41, 44
stimulant 9, 10, 16, 22, 34, 41, 47

therapy groups 44
toadstools 38
tobacco 10, 21
tolerance 12, 28, 47
track marks 28, 47
tranquillizer 32, 33
trip 36, 47

"uppers" see amphetamines

withdrawal symptoms 12, 24, 28, 32, 34, 44, 47